MASTERING THE ART OF BRUSHES

2ND EDITION

JON HAZILLA

To access audio visit:
www.halleonard.com/mylibrary

Enter Code
3784-5824-7165-8951

BERKLEE PRESS

Editor in Chief: Jonathan Feist
Senior Vice President of Online Learning and Continuing Education/CEO of Berklee Online: Debbie Cavalier
Vice President of Enrollment Marketing and Management: Mike King
Dean of Online and Continuing Education: Carin Nuernberg
Editorial Assistants: Emily Jones, Eloise Kelsey
Cover Design: artwize, www.neptunian.org
Cover Photo and Author Photo: Jonathan Feist

Jon Hazilla, Drums
John Lockwood, Bass
Recorded at Sherwood Forrest, Sept. 22, 1999
Engineered by Crit Harmon and Scott Eisenberg
Mastered by Rob Jaczko

ISBN 978-0-634-00962-4

Berklee
Press

1140 Boylston Street
Boston, MA 02215-3693 USA
(617) 747-2146

Visit Berklee Press Online at
www.berkleepress.com

Berklee Online

Study music online at
online.berklee.edu

DISTRIBUTED BY

HAL•LEONARD®

7777 W. BLUEMOUND RD. P.O. BOX 13819
MILWAUKEE, WISCONSIN 53213

Visit Hal Leonard Online
www.halleonard.com

Berklee Press, a publishing activity of Berklee College of Music, is a not-for-profit educational publisher.
Available proceeds from the sales of our products are contributed to the scholarship funds of the college.

CONTENTS

PREFACE

The art of brushes is an under-discussed topic. Drummers often approach brushes as if they were sticks. Brushes are not sticks. They have their own intrinsic nature, waiting to be fully explored by you.

There is no standard for brush notation. This makes it challenging to write about the nuances and subtle possibilities of brush performance. *Mastering the Art of Brushes* indicates brush strokes using a two-tone system (grey and black), which my students have found easy to follow.

Beyond providing simple patterns, this book will get you started using brushes and develop your brush dexterity and technique. Fundamental patterns merge with exercises to inspire your own creativity and foster your own brush style.

I have taught brushes to many beginning drummers, even before they have mastered basic strokes and fills. With no preconceived ideas about brushes, they find that the possibilities are endless.

PREFACE TO THE SECOND EDITION

A lot has changed since I first wrote those introductory words in the first edition of *Mastering the Art of Brushes*. There is a shrinking pool of opportunities to play brushes in the context of a classic jazz ensemble setting—trio, quartet, or larger ensemble. However, there is an expanding ocean of creative opportunities to play and explore brushes in new genres, styles, and non-traditional settings. Folk rock à la Norah Jones, singer-songwriter, hip-hop, and global fusion (playing a cajón with brushes) are all new exciting possibilities that have evolved since 2000. The possibilities and combinations are limitless.

What has not changed is the need to understand, practice, and study the historic arc of brushes from their inception/creation in the 1920s and '30s as fly swatters to the aforementioned cajón (a traditional Peruvian hand drum), which is now sometimes played with brushes and a bass-drum pedal played with the heel.

You cannot understand the present without knowing the past, and you cannot expand upon all of the unexplored patterns and grooves starting only from the present.

Although the patterns presented here are tradition-based, they offer a strong foundation for your starting point. These concepts and exercises will evaporate any preconceived stylistic boundaries and allow you to create and be a part of the future generations of great brush players.

So, approach brushes with an open mind. Have fun, and "brush on out of here."

ABOUT THE AUDIO

To access the accompanying audio, go to www.halleonard.com/mylibrary and enter the code found on the first page of this book. This will grant you instant access to every example. Examples with accompanying audio are marked with an audio icon.

ACKNOWLEDGMENTS

Do people understand your artwork?
> *"In the beginning, a few; in the end, the same few."*
>
> —Pablo Picasso

I would like to thank Tony Monforte, my first drum teacher ("Remember Your ROOTS!"); Mel "Brushes" Brown, who taught me everything I know about brushes; and Jeff Hamilton, who reminded me of everything I don't know about brushes. Thanks also to Debbie Cavalier at Berklee Press, who started and supported the first edition, and Jonathan Feist who continues to believe in me in the second edition. Thanks to Carol at Regal Tip, Neil Grover at Grover Drums, Adam at Remo, Torab Majlesi at Classic Cymbals in Italy, and to Jerry Kalaf, John Lockwood, David Franz, and Dave Johnstone. I want to thank my colleagues John Ramsay, Joe Hunt, and Skip Hadden for their valuable insights and suggestions; Rob Jaczko (you're a genius!); Douglas Tran (owner of All Seasons Table in Malden, MA); and John Pierce, leader of A.S.T. trio, for giving me a place to refine my brush skills—for over nine years!

Finally, thank you to all of my students who inspire me to practice even more, and to my family.

Love to you all.

INTRODUCTION

This book is divided into three parts: Concepts, Patterns, and Technique.

Concepts provides the theory behind the practice of playing with brushes. Refer to the Concepts section when practicing the Patterns and Technique sections. Understanding the concepts can help you develop greater skill in improvisation, balance out one-hand dominance, and allow you to explore and create patterns that are new and personal.

Patterns contains patterns for brush movement and technique. Approach and study the patterns as you would a classic rock beat or a traditional samba. The strokes are part- and rhythm-specific. If your left hand is supposed to play circles emphasizing beats 2 and 4, then think of that as your backbeat. Don't change the shape or the rhythm.

Technique is a series of technical exercises modeled after the genius of Alan Dawson and Joe Morello. The exercises are designed to help you develop the strokes and the overall flow. When practicing them, I recommend that you combine the suggested patterns with your own patterns. Even though you may think you have mastered a certain stroke, exploring and working through the various exercises will help you expand the improvisational nature of your filling and comping.

Since the first edition of *Mastering the Art of Brushes*, I have spent countless hours practicing, discovering, teaching, and refining specific technical exercises to support the development of lateral motion with brushes. I have added three new exercises to this section: Wrist Calisthenics, The Paradiddle-Diddle Morph Collapse, and Ostinato Studies. These new technical exercises, combined with the Wrist Table, will enhance your lateral vocabulary and rewire your stick mentality "frame of mind," when you play brushes.

At all times, be mindful of the sound you are achieving. Saxophonists and violinists are always concerned with their tone. Percussionists should be also.

This book is dedicated to all the great brushers out there: Denzil Best, PaPa Jo Jones, Buddy Rich, Louie Bellson, Shadow Wilson, Specs Wright, Vernel Fournier, Kenny Clarke, Philly Joe Jones, Art Taylor, Joe Hunt, Chico Hamilton, Larry Bunker, Ed Thigpen, Shelly Manne, Elvin Jones, Marty Morrel, Mel Brown, Jeff Hamilton, Kenny Washington, Lewis Nash, Clayton Cameron, Joe LaBarbera, Ulysses Owens Jr., Ali Jackson, Paulo Braga, Neal Smith, Billy Kilson, Terri Lyne Carrington, Ralph Peterson, Yoron Israel, Casey Scheuerell, Jim Saporito, and then some.

Concepts

Frequently, students learn to play one pattern and then nothing more. The learned pattern may sound stiff and lack groove. The students do not know how to make it sound better or fill within the pattern.

The concepts in this section are designed to help you improve your patterns and make them sound better. They can also help strengthen your ability to embellish and fill within a pattern without disrupting the time flow or groove. Studying the concepts will also help you develop brush dexterity and coordination. The concepts in this section are an essential part of the book. Experiment with them and use them when you practice the patterns and techniques in later sections.

10 CONCEPTS

1. Practice all strokes using only your hands and fingertips on the drum (without brushes).
2. Traditional grip is recommended when you hold the brushes.
3. Grip the brush 2 inches from the wires.
4. Play the tips of the brushes.
5. Use your feet to feather the bass, and play the hi-hat for bottom and support.
6. Experiment with counterclockwise or less familiar motions.
7. Each hand should play a discernible rhythm unless you want color or texture.
8. Use shape to define strokes and rhythm.
9. Create variations of shape to imply the same rhythm.
10. Use the shape to imply fills, accents, and metric modulation.

CONCEPT 1

Practice all strokes using only your hands and fingertips on the drum (without brushes).

It is much easier to capture the shape and flow of a pattern with your hands. Once you have perfected the stroke, it is easier to move to the brushes.

CONCEPT 2

Traditional grip is recommended when you hold the brushes.

When using brushes, the traditional grip is superior to the matched grip for strokes and fills. Matched grip inhibits and limits maximum range and freedom for some patterns. Traditional grip gives you a greater range of motion and the freedom to do patterns and fills.

CONCEPT 3

Grip the brush 2 inches from the wires.

Although this might be considered a choked grip, it gives you better control for shading and accenting specific strokes, fills, and patterns. The farther your grip is from the wires, the less control you will have; you will have more of the brush working for you, but less control over it.

CONCEPT 4

Play the tips of the brushes.

When playing patterns or time, play on the tips of your brushes, holding the brushes at a 30-degree angle to the snare. Otherwise, you will lose the contrast that is essential for pulse, nuance, and soft shadings in accenting, embellishing, and filling. A lower angle gives you a more legato sound. A higher angle gives you a more staccato sound.

CONCEPT 5

Use your feet to feather the bass, and play the hi-hat for bottom and support.

Brushes can be less rhythmically defined and need greater support, definition, and bottom than sticks. When using brushes, feather the bass drum and use the hi-hat to provide bottom and support. Feathering the bass lets you play very soft quarter notes or half notes to provide bottom and support, with the bass player in a lower harmonic range. However, the hi-hat can overpower the brushes, particularly on ballads where you need a softer execution or 1/4 foot stroke (cymbals 1/2 inch apart).

CONCEPT 6

Experiment with counterclockwise or less familiar motions.

To develop fluidity and facility with brushes, practice less familiar motions. This will help you strengthen the strokes that feel natural or comfortable. It is the best way to discover new strokes and develop variations on established patterns.

CONCEPT 7

Each hand should play a discernible rhythm unless you want color or texture.

Brushes are so soft that the subtlety of what you are playing (the pattern) can be lost or less precise unless each hand is playing a shape that relates to a rhythm. White noise, texture, and color may be desirable or appropriate within certain sections of tunes. The defined musical outcome determines how strongly you want to imply time, or if one or both hands are actively shading time, color, and textures.

CONCEPT 8

Use shape to define strokes and rhythm.

Use recognizable shapes to begin experimenting with strokes and patterns. Circles, heart shapes, and X's are three shapes that you can use with almost all tempos and grooves (ballads, medium, fast, Latin).

CONCEPT 9

Create variations of shape to imply the same rhythm.

To create greater fluidity between transitional strokes, and to discover your own personal strokes, experiment creating variations of shapes to imply a rhythm. Transitional strokes include circles, heart shapes, and X's. They may be played as quarter notes, eighth notes, triplets, sixteenth notes, and so forth. The rhythm table in the Techniques section develops this concept more. Do not let shape guide your sound. Let sound guide your shape. Experiment. Be creative.

CONCEPT 10

Use the shape to imply fills, accents, and metric modulation.

When creating and maintaining a time feel and flow, brushes are similar to sticks. For example, when playing time with sticks, the right hand predominantly stays on the ride cymbal to create a cushion. The left hand and right foot are used in supportive, accent roles underneath the ride cymbal. When playing time with brushes, for the most part, both hands are on the snare together. It may be disruptive to the overall time feel or cushion if either hand leaves the snare often. It is easier to embellish, accent, and fill within the original stroke or pattern by maintaining the original shape. The rhythm table and coordination exercises strengthen this concept further.

PART II

Patterns

As you begin practicing and playing the patterns, you may notice a similarity in sound between them. That is great! Producing a similar-sounding pattern with different shapes (Concept 9) helps you begin to develop your brush technique. The more emphasis you put on motion and shape to produce the same sound, the more easily you will develop fluidity with the brushes. When the sound remains constant, you can begin to explore more shapes and develop a variety of motions. With practice, your control, flexibility, and sense of flow in all directions on the drum will be greatly enhanced.

Included with each pattern is a rhythm. Following this rhythm will help you play the desired sound and duration for each hand. Some patterns have more than one rhythm indicated. If there is a rhythmic variation, such as for the Heart Shape, practice each pattern separately.

I urge you to practice all of the patterns with the accompanying tracks or any recorded performance that has a simple, clearly defined time feel (for example, Miles Davis's *Kind of Blue*). It is not necessary to practice the patterns with a recording that has brushes. The simpler the music, the easier it will be for you to concentrate on your stroke and the sound you are getting.

If you do not have a snare drum to practice on, try using an old album cover, or something of a similar texture. Choose something lightweight, easy to play on, not too loud, and similar in size to a snare head.

Brushes are not sticks, and I strongly encourage you to approach playing brushes with lateral motion. Stick technique is vertical and still may be used when playing brushes; it's unavoidable. But to engage fully in all possibilities and nuances that brushes have to offer, think of using the broad "fan" of the brush to explore an unlimited palette of sounds, textures, and colors. Literally, think of using brushes as painting pictures on a canvas. With sticks, it would be much more difficult to paint a picture.

BRUSH STROKES KEY

We use the following conventions for brush diagrams in this book.

	Left Hand (L.H.)	Right Hand (R.H.)
On Drum	▬▬▬▬	▬▬▬▬
Off Drum	▬ ▬ ▬ ▬	▬ ▬ ▬ ▬
Tap	●▬▬	●▬▬
Tap Rhythm	f ▲ mf ▲ p ▴	f ▲ mf ▲ p ▴

Note: f = forte (loud); mf = mezzo forte (medium loud); p = piano (soft)

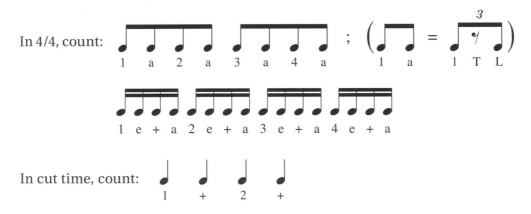

- **Tap:** *Taps* are used mostly within patterns to add a soft pulse at the beginning or end of a stroke. The brush is never entirely lifted *off* the drum. The tap helps define the pulse within the pattern.
- **Tap Rhythm:** A clean-attack *tap rhythm* (not part of the stroke itself) is made by lifting the entire brush off the drumhead and articulating the rhythm as indicated. The *tap rhythm* is part of the actual pattern and must be cleanly articulated to complete the full sound/rhythm of the intended pattern. The size of the triangle corresponds to the dynamic that should be played for each note.

Pay special attention to the rhythm for each pattern. This will help clarify the difference.

DRUM AND BASS PLAY-ALONG TRACKS

The play-along tracks with drum and bass let you hear the pattern first. This will help you capture the phrase markings, accents, and dynamics that appear in the grey box below each pattern. It will also give you room to experiment with your own shapes to create the same *sound* (Concept 9).

In each track, the drums play the brush pattern in a four-bar phrase(s). The bass and drums play together for the next phrase(s), then the drums drop out, allowing you to practice keeping the flow and groove in a musical context.

BALLADS

 ## Circles

2

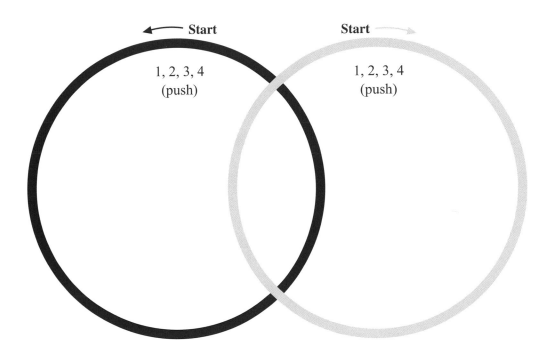

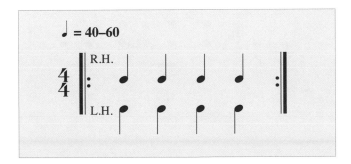

Instructions

Starting at twelve o'clock, press both brushes fully into the drumhead for a quarter-note rhythm.

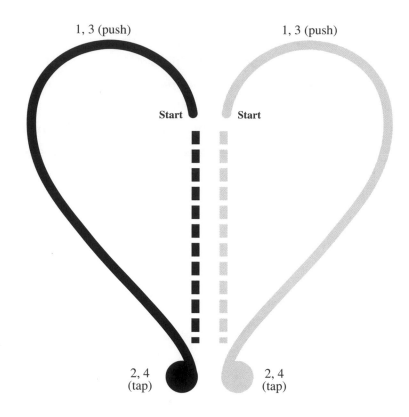

Heart Shape

3

1, 3 (push)　　　　　　1, 3 (push)

Start　　Start

2, 4
(tap)　　　　2, 4
(tap)

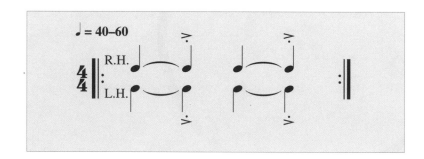

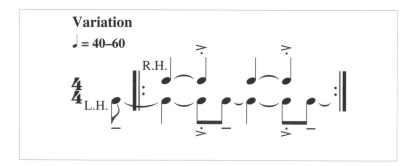

Instructions

On the start, cut both hands in 45-degree angles on beats 1 and 3. On beats 2
and 4, give a slight tap with both hands.

　　Note: the basic rhythm is on the recording.

　　As a variation, the left hand can anticipate beats 1 and 3 by an eighth note.

Half Circles

4

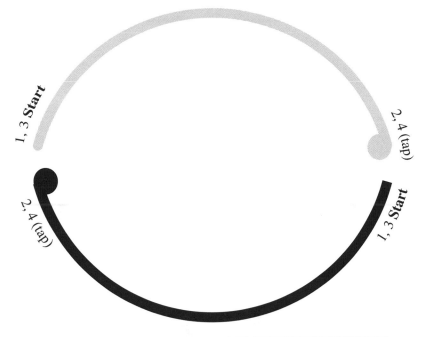

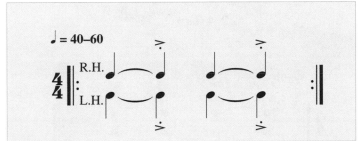

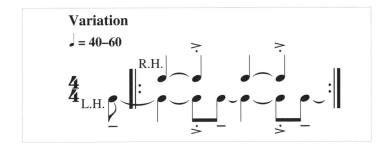

Instructions

There are three hand variations to practice:

1. Right hand over left hand starting position =

2. Left hand over right hand starting position =

3. Alternating every two beats; right over left, left over right =

Attacks in both hands on beats 1 and 3 should not be heard. Stroke should blend into the drumhead at a 45-degree angle. Both hands lift off the drum after completing a half circle and return to the starting position for beats 3 and 4.

As a variation, the left hand can anticipate beats 1 and 3 by an eighth note.

Shoulder Stroke

5

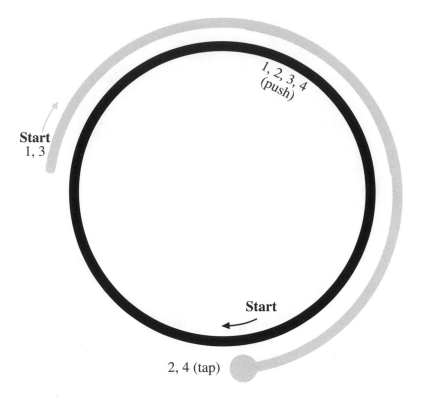

Instructions

The right hand should come in from your left shoulder and blend in at a 45-degree angle. The right hand lifts off the drum after (tap beat 2) and returns to the starting position for beat 3.

As a variation, the left hand can anticipate beats 1 and 3 by an eighth note.

MEDIUM TEMPOS

 ### The Standard

6

This is the most fundamental brush pattern. It can be used for a variety of tempos.

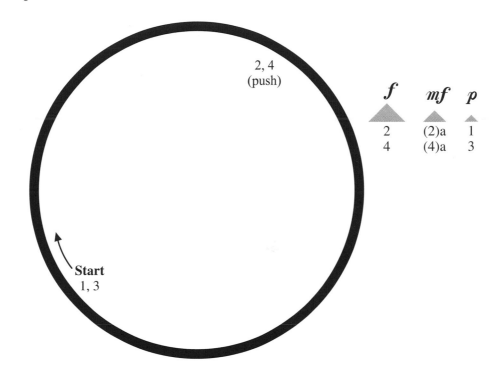

2, 4
(push)

f   *mf*   *p*

2   (2)a   1
4   (4)a   3

Start
1, 3

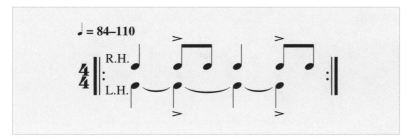

Instructions

The right hand can stay on one side of the drum without crossing over. Practice the left hand as a half-note rhythm (one full circle for two beats) with a legato feel. Also practice the left hand in a counterclockwise direction.

Windshield Wiper

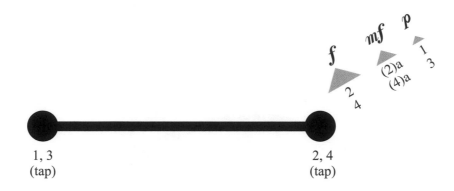

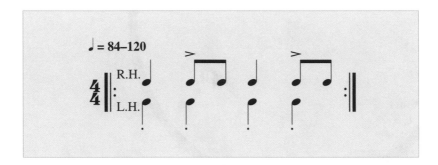

Instructions

The right hand can stay on one side or cross over. The left hand must stop at each side of the drum for a more staccato rhythm.

Elvin's Left-Hand Lead

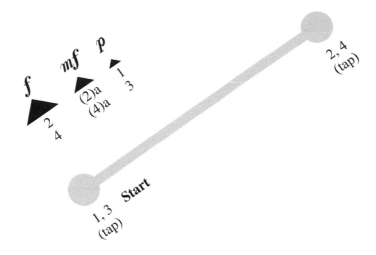

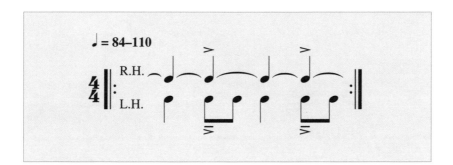

Instructions

This stroke has many possibilities. If you play the right hand side to side, rather than in a long oval, you can cross the left hand over.

🔊 Philly Joe Special
9

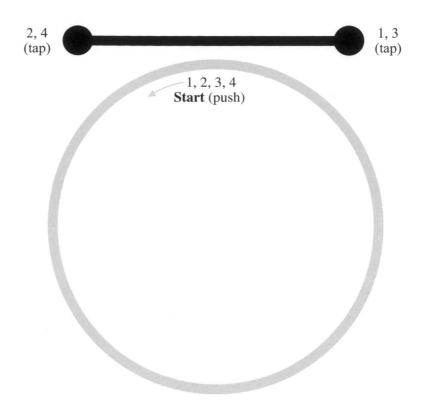

2, 4
(tap)

1, 3
(tap)

1, 2, 3, 4
Start (push)

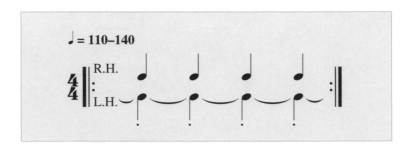

♩ = 110–140

R.H.
4/4
L.H.

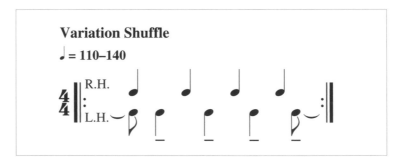

Variation Shuffle

♩ = 110–140

R.H.
4/4
L.H.

Instructions

The right hand has a very strong, smooth, legato feel. The left hand has a staccato, abrupt feel.

UP TEMPO

 The Cheat

10

In $\frac{4}{4}$ Time

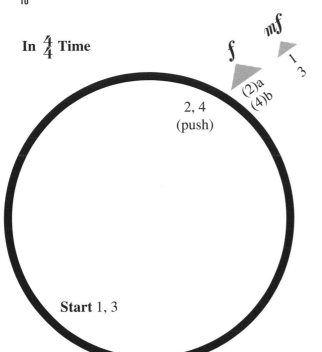

2, 4
(push)

Start 1, 3

In ¢ Time

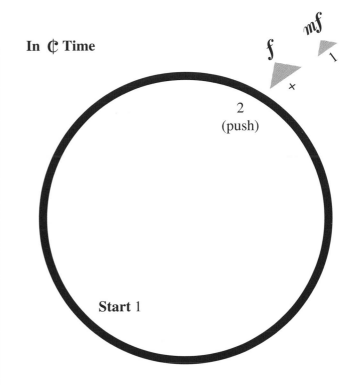

2
(push)

Start 1

Common Time

♩ = 300–400

Cut Time

𝅗𝅥 = 150–200

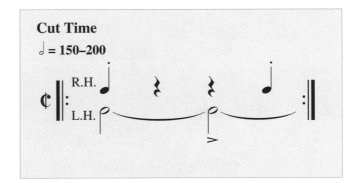

Instructions

Practice the left hand in both directions (clockwise and counterclockwise). It must lock in with the left foot. Count in cut time ("1+2+") to hear and see how it relates to a fast 4/4 time (1, 2, 3, 4). In cut time, the left foot comes down on the "ands" (+). The right hand can be played either staccato or legato (being left on the drum longer, slightly dragging on beat 1).

The Wiper Stop

11

In 4/4 Time

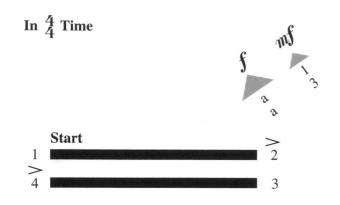

In ¢ Time

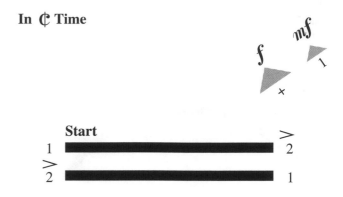

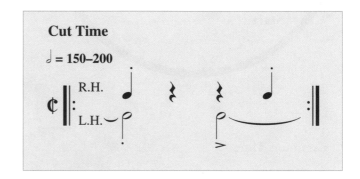

Instructions

Play the left hand as staccato as possible, stopping at each side of the drum. The left hand traces over itself and returns to the starting position after two measures in cut time.

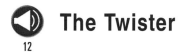

The Twister

In $\frac{4}{4}$ Time

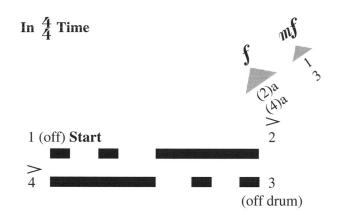

In ¢ Time

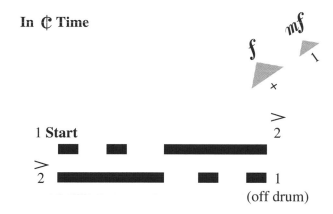

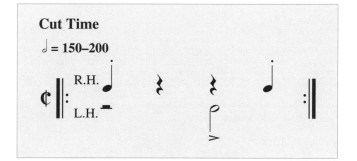

Common Time

♩ = 300–400

Cut Time

♩ = 150–200

Instructions

This is a variation of the Wiper Stop stroke. The left hand is off the drum to start. Lift the left hand and slightly twist the wrist for greater clarity. This pattern is good for ultra fast tempos. The left hand returns to the starting position after two measures in cut time.

Haz's Triplet

13

In $\frac{4}{4}$ Time

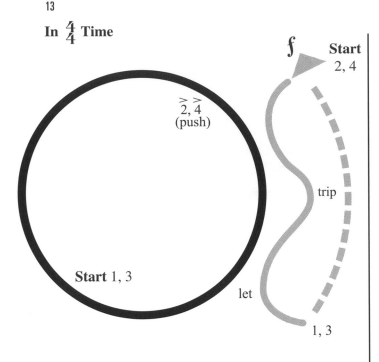

In ¢ Time

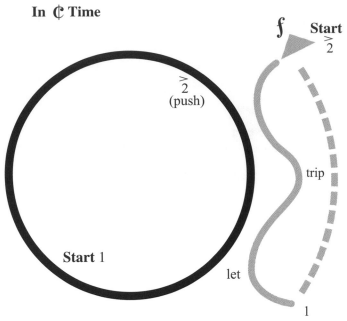

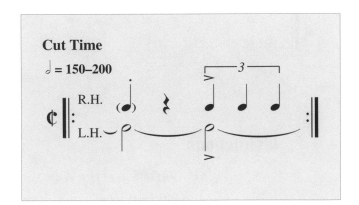

Instructions

Start this stroke with the right hand on beat 2. The common-time notation works great at medium tempos too.

14

South Philly Special

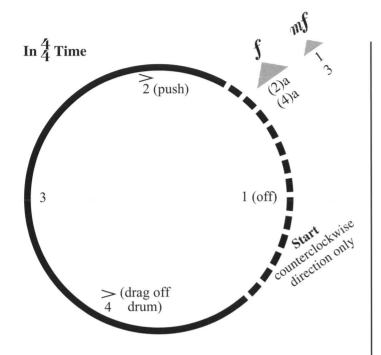

In $\frac{4}{4}$ Time

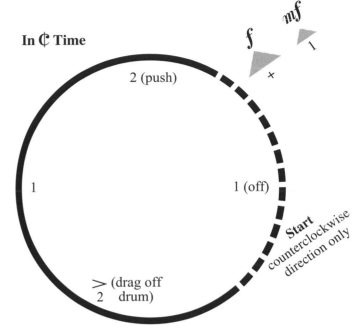

In ₵ Time

Common Time

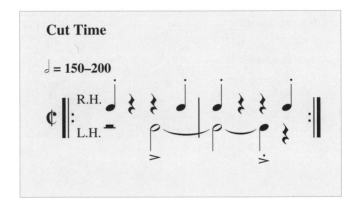

Cut Time

Instructions

This is a great visual stroke. It is easy to slip back and forth between this and the Cheat. It takes two bars to complete the circle in cut time. The left hand works only in a counterclockwise motion.

The Guiro Philly Special

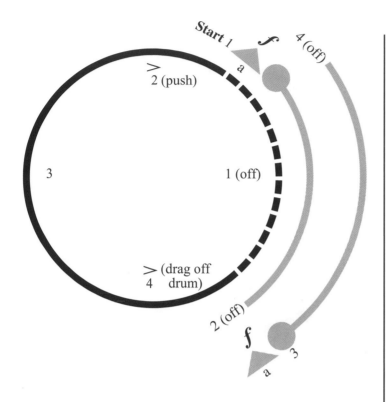

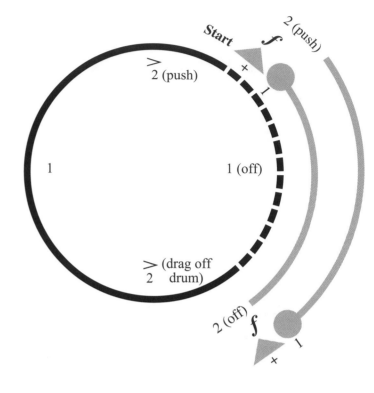

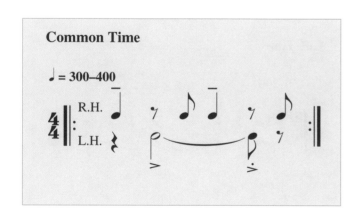

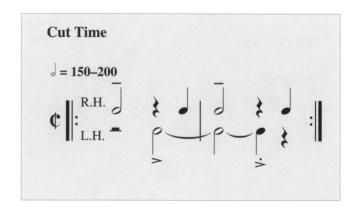

Instructions

At the broken line, keep the right hand in the same direction as the left hand. Practice the right hand separately. It should sound like a guiro. The left hand part is identical to that of the South Philly Special.

SPECIAL STROKES

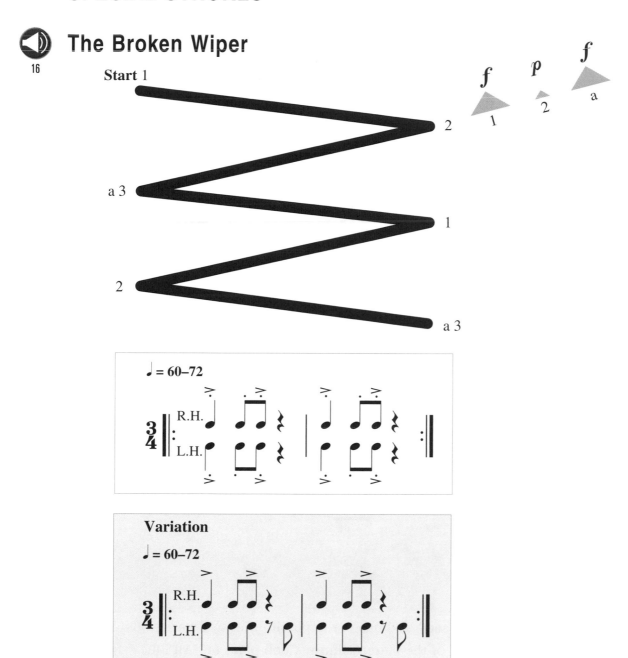

The Broken Wiper

16

Instructions

This is a two-bar pattern. Start this stroke with a very articulated staccato approach. Both hands emphasize the dotted-quarter-note feel in 3/4. When you are comfortable with the sound and feel of the stroke, you can cross the right hand over the left hand on the opposite side of the drum from the left hand. The left hand never leaves the drum.

As a variation, the left hand can add an extra sweep on beat 3a. You can use this same two-bar rhythmic pattern by alternating the shapes to circles or X's, and playing them as unison. (The left-hand motion is from side to side, tracing over itself.)

Cobb's All Blues

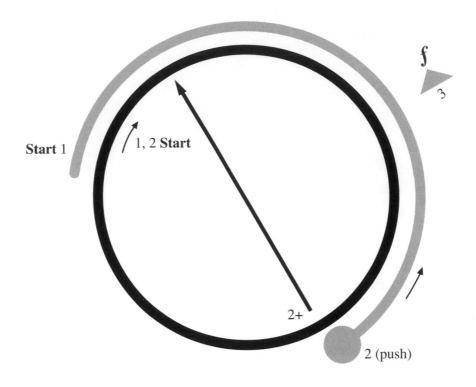

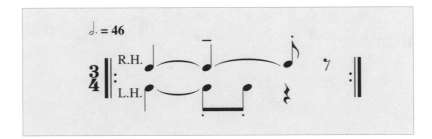

Instructions

This stroke is only a seed and has many possibilities and variations. It is reminiscent in sound of the pattern Jimmy Cobb plays on "All Blues" from Miles Davis's recording *Kind of Blue*.

Right hand starts at 9 o'clock with the tip of the brush and moves clockwise to 5 o'clock. Beat 2, tap and push in the opposite direction, with all of the wires on the head. On beat 3, lift the brush and play a short tap rhythm back at 2 o'clock.

Left hand starts inside the right hand at 9 o'clock. Make a complete small clockwise circle, ending on beat 2 at 9 o'clock. Lift the brush and, on the "and" of beat 2, play a straight line/short-staccato sweep across the center of the drumhead.

On the Edge

17

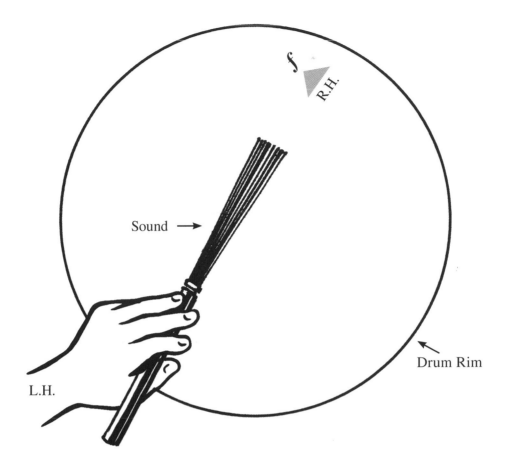

Instructions

Placement of the left hand is critical to getting the correct sound. The palm of the left hand must rest on the rim of the drum and not move, to create a 25-degree angle of brush. The rhythm is better articulated with a slapping motion of fingers. The sound comes from one inch of the rubber and one inch of the wire. Do not take the brush or the hand off of the drum.

As a variation, the right hand can stay in one place, or you can play the right-hand brush directly on the left-hand brush for a funkier groove. This pattern works well with any samba pattern, especially very fast sambas.

18

The Bagby

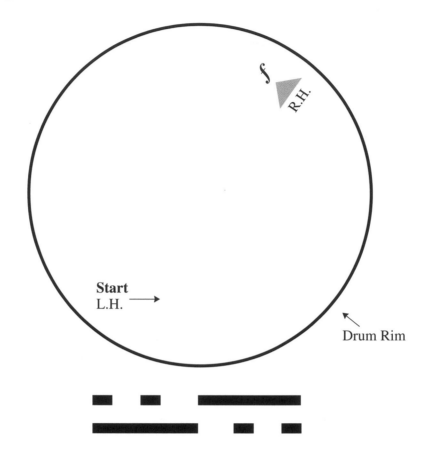

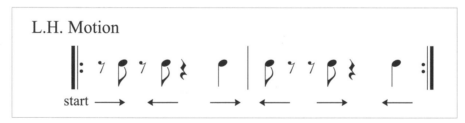

Instructions

The left-hand motion is exactly the same as The Twister. Twist the left wrist and lift it off the drum as you go back and forth. The rhythm is articulated by the fresh attack and sweep of each note as you follow the direction of the arrows. The right hand stays in one place.

Any samba rhythm can work as long as you coordinate the left-hand motion with any rhythm. This stroke works very well for medium sambas where a thicker sound is desired.

BASS PLAY-ALONG TRACKS

Audio tracks 19 to 23 contain solo bass grooves in a variety of tempos and styles. Practice the brush patterns with the corresponding bass grooves; i.e., Ballad Strokes with track 19, Ballad Tempo.

For an added challenge, try to play some of the brush patterns with the bass grooves at different tempos; e.g., Circles (which is a ballad pattern) with track 20, Medium Tempo.

It is not recommended to practice Section III's Coordination Exercises with the bass play-along tracks.

 Ballad Tempo
19

 Medium Tempo
20

 Up-Tempo
21

 Specialty Strokes: 3/4 Tempo
22

 Specialty Strokes: Samba
23

Technique

RHYTHM TABLE FOR WRIST DEVELOPMENT

After working through all of the patterns, you can begin to work on increasing your dexterity with brushes. The rhythm table and motion exercises in this section are designed to help you strengthen your skill with the patterns, and blend fills and accents that complement the patterns.

With brushes, it is important to use the wrist, rather than the elbow for lateral motion. Using the wrist shortens the motion, giving you better control to articulate the rhythms of the stroke or fill more clearly.

Practice the rhythm table with one hand at a time *separately*, then with both hands together *unison*, and finally *alternating* hands. There are two basic shapes to practice: circles and straight lines. Practice circles in both clockwise and counterclockwise motion. Practice the rhythmic groupings first in order, then shift to different groupings in any order.

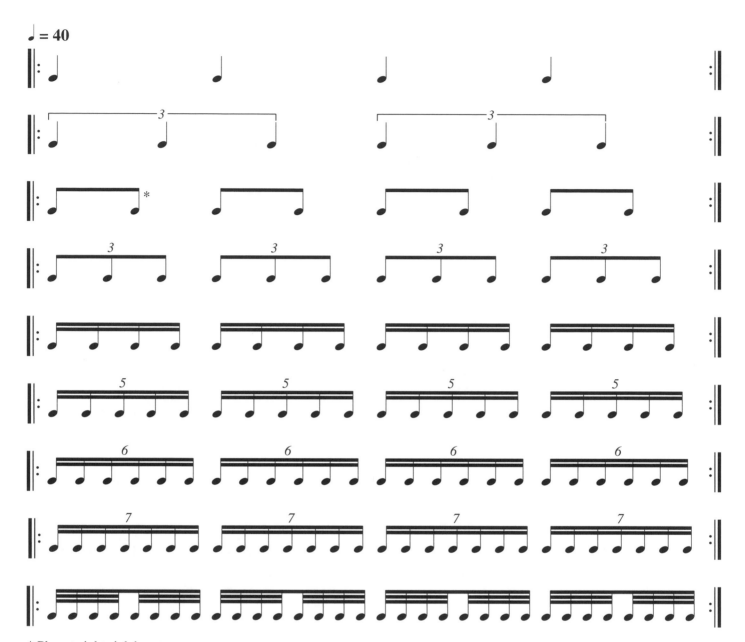

* Play straight eighth notes.

Separately

You can start the patterns anywhere, though I recommend at 12:00.

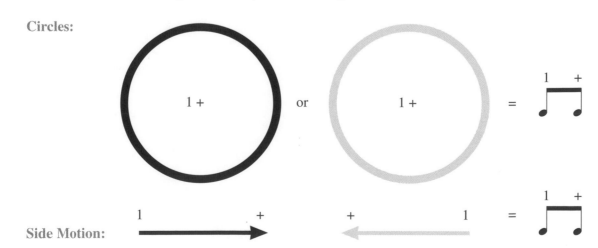

Unison

Circles:

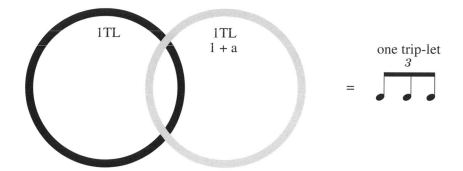

Side Motion:

1TL = one trip-let

Alternating

Circles:

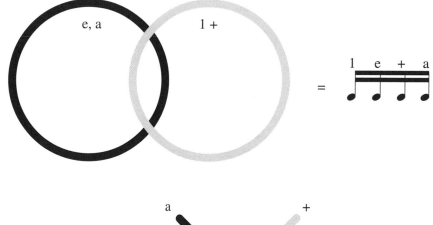

Side Motion: (can become X shape)

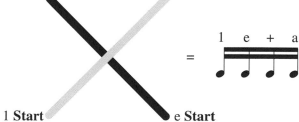

The right hand pushes underneath the left hand never leaving the drum. Additional hand rhythms and combinations to augment your brush dexterity with this exercise may be found by using the first section of *Stick Control* by George Stone or *Odd Meter Calisthenics* by Mitchell Peters.

WRIST CALISTHENICS

This is a basic warm-up exercise that combines single strokes with double strokes. The premise is to reintroduce single strokes and doubles strokes with lateral motion instead of a vertical stick approach. It is best to start slowly, with the right hand at one o'clock moving to seven o'clock and back. The left hand starts at eleven o'clock and moves to five o'clock. For the single strokes, both hands alternate, starting the first stroke at the top and the return stroke at the bottom. In double strokes, both hands start and finish at the top of the drum head. Both hands should touch the head in an identical length of sweep and sound. Experiment with both!

Review the Concepts section for suggestions on grip and angle of the brush. The slower the tempo, the longer the brush will stay on the head (legato). Faster tempos will generate a more staccato sound. I encourage you to experiment with both "sounds" and "tempos" to develop a broad range of sensitivity in touch and nuance. I also encourage you, when practicing slowly, to extend your stroke beyond the rim/edge of the drum, remaining parallel to the head. This exaggerated motion will reinforce lateral motion.

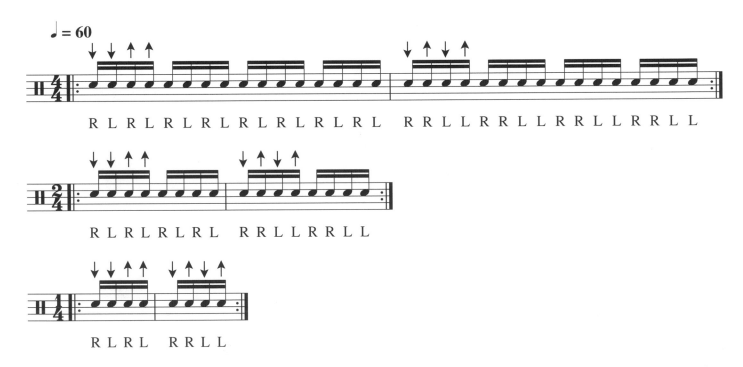

The Paradiddle-Morph Collapse

This is a very challenging exercise because the lead hand changes every measure, and the first beat of each measure *alternates* going from the top to the bottom of the drum, then bottom to top. The start and stop points are the same:

- Right hand starts at one o'clock and finishes at seven o'clock.
- Left hand starts at eleven o'clock and finishes at five.

The golden rule is each hand stays in position (either top or bottom) and moves from that position only when it is time for the next stroke. There is no wasted motion without incorporating a returning stroke.

Reminder: Both hands should touch the drum head in an identical length of sweep and sound. Experiment with both!

Once you have mastered the above exercise, you can try combining long legato sweeps as accents on the first beat of each paradiddle-diddle and playing the remaining notes staccato. Also practice the turn-around paradiddle either straight or swing.

Ostinato Studies

In the early 1980s, I had the honor to study with Joe Morello for three years. It serendipitously coincided with the release of his classic book *Master Studies*. I have practiced *Master Studies* cover-to-cover countless times.

Joe described the book as topical and not sequential, and he encouraged me to isolate and fully master specific sections. I was drawn to the ostinato section. It made simple sense that the benefits I derived from practicing with sticks could be translated to brushes and lateral motion.

The three ostinatos I have included here are the ones that I use the most. Obviously, there are countless others. I recommend that you begin by isolating each hand and doing reps or counts (e.g., RR LL) twenty-five times, then RR RR LL LL twenty-five times, etc.

When you have developed some endurance, play these ostinatos with one hand, and with the other, read the melodies in the back of this book (page 35). Then switch hands: the second hand plays the ostinato while the first one reads.

I recommend that you first practice the melody as all eighth notes, using a vertical tapping motion. When you have worked out the coordination, play the actual note values: eighth notes are now a staccato sweep, and longer note values (tied eighth notes, quarter notes, dotted quarters, half notes) are legato sweeps, alternating in both directions.

Practice eighth-note ostinatos and melodies as straight and swing. For sixteenth-note melodies, Gary Chester's *The New Breed* works great.

For more advanced study, think of either hand as an ostinato within a certain style, that you normally would play on hi-hat or ride cymbal (e.g., rock eighth note, funk sixteenth, 12/8 blues/gospel). Instead, play the ostinato on the snare (RH). The other hand (LH) plays "taps" on beats 2 and 4 as a backbeat. Bass drum can play the melody. More advanced, the left hand can play short notes (eighth notes) while the bass drum plays all long notes (tied eighths, quarters, dotted quarters, half notes). This works well in a cut-time feel or half-time funk feel.

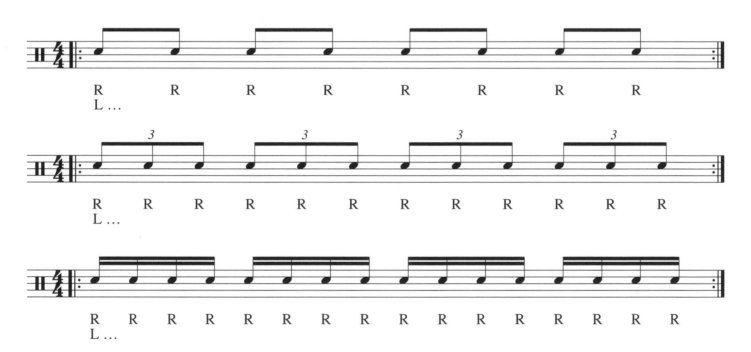

COORDINATION EXERCISES

There are nine coordination exercises to practice after you have mastered the patterns. Use the nine exercises in this section to embellish the patterns with comping figures. The exercises will help you develop a greater range of independence in each pattern. Practice the left hand as a quarter-note rhythm and a half-note rhythm (for example, 2, 3, 4).

There are five melody heads to use for each of these exercises starting on page 40. Each exercise indicates a hand or foot to play the melody. Some exercises include feathering bass drum and hi-hat on beats 2 and 4.

Nine Exercises

Exercise 1

26

Hand-to-hand triplets as circles. Each hand plays a quarter-note triplet. When combined, the rhythm is:

Now read the melodic exercises accenting the melody. Make sure you start the exercise with the left hand as well as the right.

Exercise 2

27

L.H. = Circles clockwise; circles counterclockwise
R.H. = Play melody; stay on right side of drum

Exercise 3

28

L.H. = Circles clockwise; circles counterclockwise
R.H. = ♩ ♫ ♩ ♫ = Standard stroke
R.F. = Play melody

Exercise 4

29

L.H. = Circles clockwise; circles counterclockwise
R.H. = Play all short notes (eighth notes) in melody; stay on one side of drum = ♪
R.F. = Play all long notes (tied eighth notes and longer) in melody = ♪‿♩ ♩‿♩. ♩

Exercise 5

30

R.H. = ♩ ♩ ♩ ♩ = Elvin's Left-Hand Lead stroke
L.H. = Play melody

Exercise 6

31

R.H. = ♩ ♩ ♩ ♩ = Elvin's Left-Hand Lead stroke
L.H. = ♩ ♫ ♩ ♫ = Elvin's Left-Hand Lead stroke
R.F. = Play melody

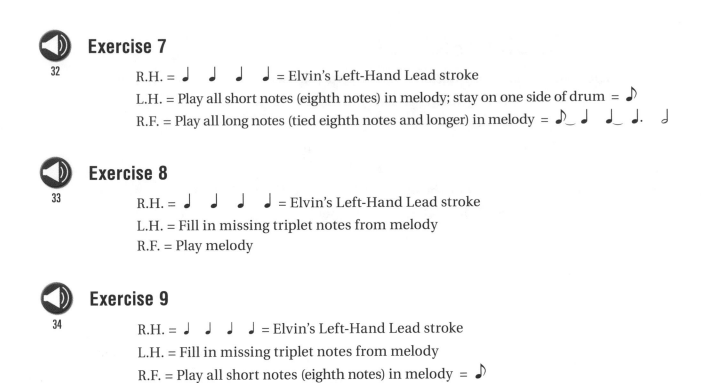

Exercise 7

32

R.H. = ♩ ♩ ♩ ♩ = Elvin's Left-Hand Lead stroke

L.H. = Play all short notes (eighth notes) in melody; stay on one side of drum = ♪

R.F. = Play all long notes (tied eighth notes and longer) in melody = ♪‿♩ ♩‿♩. ♩

Exercise 8

33

R.H. = ♩ ♩ ♩ ♩ = Elvin's Left-Hand Lead stroke

L.H. = Fill in missing triplet notes from melody

R.F. = Play melody

Exercise 9

34

R.H. = ♩ ♩ ♩ ♩ = Elvin's Left-Hand Lead stroke

L.H. = Fill in missing triplet notes from melody

R.F. = Play all short notes (eighth notes) in melody = ♪

L.F. = Play all long notes (tied eighth notes and longer) in melody = ♪‿♩ ♩‿♩. ♩

MELODY HEADS FOR THE EXERCISES

The melody heads are based on actual tunes. The first three are famous blues heads, the last two are 32 bars, AABA tunes. There are one or two rhythm modifications in each example. I suggest playing the melodies straight without any embellishments or applying the suggested coordination exercises. When you are comfortable, start with the first exercise and gradually work through all nine exercises. Pay special attention, and be aware of the phrasing and resolution points within the structure of each tune.

Flat Billie

The Chase

A.C.

Ring a Ding

No Apology

APPENDIX A. TYPES OF BRUSHES

All brushes are not created equal. Before you buy brushes, take them out of the container to inspect them. Make sure that they retract easily and that the shank of the brush is made of a material that feels good in your hands. Plastic corrugated shanks, metal, and rubber are materials that, with repeated use, may feel uncomfortable. Check the balance and weight to see if they are light enough to play very fast tempos.

"Multi rods," "Rakes," and "Blas-Stixs" are not brushes. They offer an infinite variety for experimentation of new sound sources and color, but you should never use them as a replacement for brushes.

I recommend the Regal Tip retractable brushes. They come closest to the older Premier 555 that Philly Joe used. They are simple in construction and durable.

The new Jeff Hamilton model (made by Regal Tip), I like as well, but they take some getting used to. The shank diameter is thicker, there are fewer wires, and the gauge of the wire is thicker, which gives them a stiffer feel. This allows the brush to cut through and offer more volume and attack in a variety of musical settings.

I avoid some brushes with plastic shanks, which can be slippery and may prevent you from playing rim-flex rhythms. Some brushes are difficult to retract, even with repeated use.

APPENDIX B. DISCOGRAPHY

The following list is a discography of drummers known for their outstanding brush playing. The list, which is alphabetical by drummer, is not intended to be all inclusive. It offers some examples for you to listen to and study.

Recording	Artist	Drummer
Light As a Feather	Chick Corea	Airto (Moreira)
Fingers	Airto (Moreira)	Airto (Moreira)
Greens	Benny Green	Carl Allen
Testiflyer	Benny Green	Carl Allen
That's Right	Benny Green	Carl Allen
All Stars	Louie Bellson	Louie Bellson
Subconscious	Lee Konitz	Denzil Best
All Eliane Elias recordings with Paulo Braga	Eliane Elias	Paulo Braga
Encounters I	Jessica Williams	Mel Brown
Encounters II	Jessica Williams	Mel Brown
Trio 65	Bill Evans	Larry Bunker
The Trio of Hank Jones	Hank Jones	Kenny Clarke
Live at the Pershing Vols. I, II	Ahmad Jamal	Vernel Fournier
Gerry Mulligan Quartet	Gerry Mulligan	Chico Hamilton
Live	Jeff Hamilton	Jeff Hamilton
Bass Face	Ray Brown	Jeff Hamilton
All Jeff Hamilton Trio Recordings	Jeff Hamilton	Jeff Hamilton
Reaching Fourth	McCoy Tyner	Roy Haynes
Focus	Stan Getz	Roy Haynes
The Bitten Moon	Jon Hazilla	Jon Hazilla
Eula	John Pierce	Jon Hazilla
Form and Function	Jon Hazilla	Jon Hazilla
Soul Eyes	Jon Hazilla	Jon Hazilla
Tiny Capers	Jon Hazilla	Jon Hazilla
Nobody Else But Me	Stan Getz	Joe Hunt

Recording	Artist	Drummer
Bass	Oscar Pettiford	Ron Jefferson
Overseas	Tommy Flanagan	Elvin Jones
Upon Reflection	Hank Jones	Elvin Jones
Ballads	John Coltrane	Elvin Jones
Fresh	Jo Jones	Jo Jones
New York Jazz	Sonny Stitt	Jo Jones
Green Dolphin Street	Bill Evans	Philly Joe Jones
Time Waits	Bud Powell	Philly Joe Jones
Paris Concerts	Bill Evans	Joe La Barbera
Empathy	Bill Evans	Shelly Manne
Since We Met	Bill Evans	Marty Morell
The Tokyo Concert	Bill Evans	Marty Morell
Sea Changes	Tommy Flanagan	Lewis Nash
Out Here	Christian McBride	Ulysses Owens Jr.
Lester Young Trio	Lester Young	Buddy Rich
Garland of Red	Red Garland	Art Taylor
Amazing Bud Powell Vol. 2	Bud Powell	Art Taylor
We Take Requests	Oscar Peterson	Ed Thigpen
Jazz Poet	Tommy Flanagan	Kenny Washington
John Hicks Plays Gershwin	John Hicks	Kenny Washington
All Bill Charlap Recordings with Kenny Washington	Bill Charlap	Kenny Washington
Sonny Stitt Plays	Sonny Stitt	Shadow Wilson
Red Garland at the Prelude	Red Garland	Specs Wright

APPENDIX C. BOOKS

Drum Wisdom	Bob Moses	Modern Drummer (Dist. by Hal Leonard Corporation, 1984)
52nd Street Beat	Joe Hunt	Jamey Aebersold
Master Studies	Joe Morello	Modern Drummer (Dist. by Hal Leonard Corporation, 1983)
Odd Meter Calisthenics Exercises	Mitchell Peters	Mitchell Peters, 1973
Reading in 4/4	Louie Bellson	Warner Bros. Publications, 1993
Stick Control	George Stone	George Stone, 1935
Syncopation	Ted Reed	Ted Reed, 1953
The Art of BeBop Drumming	John Riley	Manhattan Music, 1994
The Drummer's Complete Vocabulary As Taught by Alan Dawson	John Ramsay	Manhattan Music, 1997

APPENDIX D. VIDEOS

The Art of Brushes	Clayton Cameron	Warner Bros. Publications
The Essence of Brushes	Ed Thigpen	Warner Bros. Publications

ABOUT THE AUTHOR

Photo by Jonathan Feist

Jon Hazilla has performed and/or recorded with Jo Anne Brackeen, James Williams, John Hicks, Billy Taylor, Aaron Goldberg, Ray Drummond, Ron Carter, George Garzone, Benny Golson, Billy Pierce, Steve Grossman, Larry Coryell, Kenny Wheeler, Sheila Jordan, Ran Blake, John Clayton, and Max Roach. He continues to perform in countless global festivals including the Azores, Costa Rica, Warsaw, Rome, Nice, Serbia, and Kyoto, to name a few. He is a graduate of New England Conservatory of Music.

He received a National Endowment Award in 1987, the Robert Porter Memorial Advancement Award in Education from the American Federation of Teachers in 2002, a Berklee Fellowship Grant in 2006, and the Steelgrass residency in Kauai, Hawaii in 2012.

He has produced eight recordings as a leader, and recorded over forty-five more as a sideman. Berklee Press originally published his first book *Mastering the Art of Brushes* in 2002, with its second edition in 2017. His second book, *Rhythmic Reflections on Creative Teaching*, was published by Mosaic in 2013. Hal Leonard released his DVD *Brush Control* in 2008.

Jon is cofounder of Jazz on Wheels, a volunteer group of musicians that performs free concerts at Boston public libraries for inner city children. He was a mentor for the City Music Program, volunteered for Habitat for Humanity helping victims of Hurricane Katrina, and was music facilitator for Project Common Bond serving young adults from around the world who have experienced trauma. He is a certified hospice volunteer for Asera Care Hospice. He is a Pastoral Associate at First Parish Unitarian Universalist Church in Brookline, Massachusetts, and teaches in the R. E. program. He has run over forty marathons and one ultra, and has a P.R. of 2:38.

Jon is a professor at Berklee College of Music, where he has taught since 1987. Jon's natural gift for teaching keeps him in high demand in and around Boston and worldwide.

Recordings as Leader/Co-Leader*

Soul Eyes (2016)

Chicpacity

That Bitten Moon

*C.J.Q.**

Saxabone

Tiny Capers

It Never Entered My Mind

*Kaleidoscope**

Books and Videos by Jon Hazilla

Hazilla, Jon. *Mastering the Art of Brushes: 2nd Edition.* Boston: Berklee Press, 2017. First edition 2002.

Hazilla, Jon. *Brush Control.* Milwaukee, WI: Hal Leonard Corp., 2008.

Hazilla, Jon. *Rhythmic Reflections on Creative Teaching.* Brookline, MA: Mosaic, 2013.

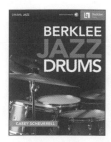 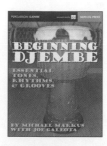     
 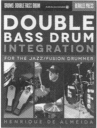     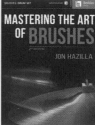 
  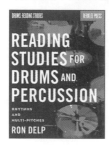    

More Fine Publications

Berklee
Press

GUITAR

BEBOP GUITAR SOLOS
by Michael Kaplan
00121703 Book $14.99

BLUES GUITAR TECHNIQUE
by Michael Williams
50449623 Book/Online Audio..........$24.99

BERKLEE GUITAR CHORD DICTIONARY
by Rick Peckham
50449546 Jazz – Book.......................$12.99
50449596 Rock – Book.......................$12.99

BERKLEE GUITAR STYLE STUDIES
by Jim Kelly
00200377 Book/Online Media..........$24.99

CLASSICAL TECHNIQUE FOR THE MODERN GUITARIST
by Kim Perlak
00148781 Book/Online Audio.............$19.99

CONTEMPORARY JAZZ GUITAR SOLOS
by Michael Kaplan
00143596 ....$16.99

CREATIVE CHORDAL HARMONY FOR GUITAR
by Mick Goodrick and Tim Miller
50449613 Book/Online Audio.............$19.99

FUNK/R&B GUITAR
by Thaddeus Hogarth
50449569 Book/Online Audio...........$19.99

GUITAR CHOP SHOP – BUILDING ROCK/METAL TECHNIQUE
by Joe Stump
50449601 Book/Online Audio............$19.99

GUITAR SWEEP PICKING
by Joe Stump
00151223 Book/Online Audio.............$19.99

INTRODUCTION TO JAZZ GUITAR
by Jane Miller
00125041 Book/Online Audio.............$19.99

JAZZ GUITAR FRETBOARD NAVIGATION
by Mark White
00154107 Book/Online Audio.............$19.99

JAZZ SWING GUITAR
by Jon Wheatley
00139935 Book/Online Audio.............$19.99

A MODERN METHOD FOR GUITAR*
by William Leavitt
Volume 1: Beginner
00137387 Book/Online Video $24.99
*Other volumes, media options, and supporting songbooks available.

A MODERN METHOD FOR GUITAR SCALES
by Larry Baione
00199318 Book......................$9.99

Berklee Press publications feature material developed at the Berklee College of Music.
To browse the complete Berklee Press Catalog, go to
www.berkleepress.com

BASS

BASS LINES
Fingerstyle Funk
by Joe Santerre
50449542 Book/CD $19.95
Metal
by David Marvuglio
00122465 Book/Online Audio............$19.99
Rock
by Joe Santerre
50449478 Book/CD $19.95

BERKLEE JAZZ BASS
by Rich Appleman, Whit Browne, and Bruce Gertz
50449636 Book/Online Audio $19.99

FUNK BASS FILLS
by Anthony Vitti
50449608 Book/CD $19.99

INSTANT BASS
by Danny Morris
50449502 Book/CD $9.99

VOICE

BELTING
by Jeannie Gagné
00124984 Book/Online Media............$19.99

THE CONTEMPORARY SINGER – 2ND ED.
by Anne Peckham
50449595 Book/Online Audio $24.99

JAZZ VOCAL IMPROVISATION
by Mili Bermejo
00159290 Book/Online Audio $19.99

TIPS FOR SINGERS
by Carolyn Wilkins
50449557 Book/CD..................$19.95

VOCAL TECHNIQUE
featuring Anne Peckham
50448038 DVD......................$19.95

VOCAL WORKOUTS FOR THE CONTEMPORARY SINGER
by Anne Peckham
50448044 Book/Online Audio..........$24.99

YOUR SINGING VOICE
by Jeannie Gagné
50449619 Book/CD $29.99

WOODWINDS/BRASS

TRUMPET SOUND EFFECTS
by Craig Pederson & Ueli Dörig
00121626 Book/Online Audio.............$14.99

SAXOPHONE SOUND EFFECTS
by Ueli Dörig
50449628 Book/Online Audio $15.99

THE TECHNIQUE OF THE FLUTE: CHORD STUDIES, RHYTHM STUDIES
by Joseph Viola
00214012 Book......................$19.99

PIANO/KEYBOARD

BERKLEE JAZZ KEYBOARD HARMONY
by Suzanna Sifter
00138874 Book/Online Audio............$24.99

BERKLEE JAZZ PIANO
by Ray Santisi
50448047 Book/Online Audio $19.99

BERKLEE JAZZ STANDARDS FOR SOLO PIANO
Arranged by Robert Christopherson, Hey Rim Jeon, Ross Ramsay, Tim Ray
00160482 Book/Online Audio............$19.99

CHORD-SCALE IMPROVISATION FOR KEYBOARD
by Ross Ramsay
50449597 Book/CD......................$19.99

CONTEMPORARY PIANO TECHNIQUE
by Stephany Tiernan
50449545 Book/DVD $29.99

HAMMOND ORGAN COMPLETE
by Dave Limina
50449479 Book/CD $24.95

JAZZ PIANO COMPING
by Suzanne Davis
50449614 Book/CD $19.99

LATIN JAZZ PIANO IMPROVISATION
by Rebecca Cline
50449649 Book/CD $24.99

SOLO JAZZ PIANO – 2ND ED.
by Neil Olmstead
50449641 Book/CD......................$39.99

DRUMS

BEGINNING DJEMBE
by Michael Markus & Joe Galeota
00148210 Book/Online Video $16.99

BERKLEE JAZZ DRUMS
by Casey Scheuerell
50449612 Book/Online Audio............$19.99

DRUM SET WARM-UPS
by Rod Morgenstein
50449465 Book........................$12.99

DRUM STUDIES
by Dave Vose
50449617 Book........................$12.99

A MANUAL FOR THE MODERN DRUMMER
by Alan Dawson & Don DeMichael
50449560 Book........................$14.99

MASTERING THE ART OF BRUSHES – 2ND EDITION
by Jon Hazilla
50449459 Book/Online Audio $19.99

PHRASING: ADVANCED RUDIMENTS FOR CREATIVE DRUMMING
by Russ Gold
00120209 Book/Online Media............$19.99

WORLD JAZZ DRUMMING
by Mark Walker
50449568 Book/CD $22.99

STRINGS/ROOTS MUSIC

BERKLEE HARP
Chords, Styles, and Improvisation for Pedal and Lever Harp
by Felice Pomeranz
00144263 Book/Online Audio $19.99

BEYOND BLUEGRASS
Beyond Bluegrass Banjo
by Dave Hollander and Matt Glaser
50449610 Book/CD $19.99

Beyond Bluegrass Mandolin
by John McGann and Matt Glaser
50449609 Book/CD $19.99

Bluegrass Fiddle and Beyond
by Matt Glaser
50449602 Book/CD $19.99

EXPLORING CLASSICAL MANDOLIN
by August Watters
00125040 Book/Online Media $19.99

FIDDLE TUNES ON JAZZ CHANGES
by Matt Glaser
00120210 Book/Online Audio $16.99

THE IRISH CELLO BOOK
by Liz Davis Maxfield
50449652 Book/CD $24.99

JAZZ UKULELE
by Abe Lagrimas, Jr.
00121624 Book/Online Audio $19.99

BERKLEE PRACTICE METHOD

GET YOUR BAND TOGETHER
With additional volumes for other instruments, plus a teacher's guide.
Bass
by Rich Appleman, John Repucci and the Berklee Faculty
50449427 Book/CD $14.95

Drum Set
by Ron Savage, Casey Scheuerell and the Berklee Faculty
50449429 Book/CD $14.95

Guitar
by Larry Baione and the Berklee Faculty
50449426 Book/CD $16.99

Keyboard
by Russell Hoffmann, Paul Schmeling and the Berklee Faculty
50449428 Book/Online Audio $14.99

WELLNESS

MANAGE YOUR STRESS AND PAIN THROUGH MUSIC
by Dr. Suzanne B. Hanser and Dr. Susan E. Mandel
50449592 Book/CD $29.99

MUSICIAN'S YOGA
by Mia Olson
50449587 Book $14.99

THE NEW MUSIC THERAPIST'S HANDBOOK – 2ND EDITION
by Dr. Suzanne B. Hanser
50449424 Book $29.95

AUTOBIOGRAPHY

LEARNING TO LISTEN: THE JAZZ JOURNEY OF GARY BURTON
by Gary Burton
00117798 Book $27.99

MUSIC THEORY/EAR TRAINING/IMPROVISATION

BEGINNING EAR TRAINING
by Gilson Schachnik
50449548 Book/CD $16.99

THE BERKLEE BOOK OF JAZZ HARMONY
by Joe Mulholland & Tom Hojnacki
00113755 Book/Online Audio $27.50

BERKLEE MUSIC THEORY – 2ND ED.
by Paul Schmeling
Rhythm, Scales Intervals
50449615 Book/Online Audio $24.99
Harmony
50449616 Book/CD $22.99

IMPROVISATION FOR CLASSICAL MUSICIANS
by Eugene Friesen with Wendy M. Friesen
50449637 Book/CD $24.99

REHARMONIZATION TECHNIQUES
by Randy Felts
50449496 Book $29.95

MUSIC BUSINESS

HOW TO GET A JOB IN THE MUSIC INDUSTRY – 3RD EDITION
by Keith Hatschek with Breanne Beseda
00130699 Book $27.99

MAKING MUSIC MAKE MONEY
by Eric Beall
50448009 Book $26.95

MUSIC LAW IN THE DIGITAL AGE – 2ND EDITION
by Allen Bargfrede
00148196 Book $19.99

MUSIC MARKETING
by Mike King
50449588 Book $24.99

PROJECT MANAGEMENT FOR MUSICIANS
by Jonathan Feist
50449659 Book $27.99

THE SELF-PROMOTING MUSICIAN – 3RD EDITION
by Peter Spellman
00119607 Book $24.99

MUSIC PRODUCTION & ENGINEERING

AUDIO MASTERING
by Jonathan Wyner
50449581 Book/CD $29.99

AUDIO POST PRODUCTION
by Mark Cross
50449627 Book $19.99

MIX MASTERS
by Maureen Droney
50448023 Book $24.95

THE SINGER-SONGWRITER'S GUIDE TO RECORDING IN THE HOME STUDIO
by Shane Adams
00148211 Book/Online Audio $16.99

UNDERSTANDING AUDIO – 2ND EDITION
by Daniel M. Thompson
00148197 Book $24.99

SONGWRITING, COMPOSING, ARRANGING

ARRANGING FOR HORNS
by Jerry Gates
00121625 Book/Online Audio $19.99

BEGINNING SONGWRITING
by Andrea Stolpe with Jan Stolpe
00138503 Book/Online Audio $19.99

BERKLEE CONTEMPORARY MUSIC NOTATION
by Jonathan Feist
00202547 Book $16.99

COMPLETE GUIDE TO FILM SCORING – 2ND ED.
by Richard Davis
50449607 .... $27.99

CONTEMPORARY COUNTERPOINT: THEORY & APPLICATION
by Beth Denisch
00147050 Book/Online Audio $19.99

JAZZ COMPOSITION
by Ted Pease
50448000 Book/Online Audio $39.99

MELODY IN SONGWRITING
by Jack Perricone
50449419 Book/CD $24.95

MODERN JAZZ VOICINGS
by Ted Pease and Ken Pullig
50449485 Book/Online Audio $24.99

MUSIC COMPOSITION FOR FILM AND TELEVISION
by Lalo Schifrin
50449604 Book $34.99

MUSIC NOTATION
PREPARING SCORES AND PARTS
by Matthew Nicholl and Richard Grudzinski
50449540 Book $16.99

MUSIC NOTATION
THEORY AND TECHNIQUE FOR MUSIC NOTATION
by Mark McGrain
50449399 Book $24.95

POPULAR LYRIC WRITING
by Andrea Stolpe
50449553 Book $15.99

SONGWRITING: ESSENTIAL GUIDE
Lyric and Form Structure
by Pat Pattison
50481582 Book $16.99

Rhyming
by Pat Pattison
00124366   2nd Ed. Book $17.99

SONGWRITING STRATEGIES
by Mark Simos
50449621 Book $22.99

THE SONGWRITER'S WORKSHOP
Harmony
by Jimmy Kachulis
50449519 Book/Online Audio $29.99

Melody
by Jimmy Kachulis
50449518 Book/CD $24.99

HAL•LEONARD®